THE LITTLE BOOK OF

quick fixes
FOR DESIGNING YOUR OUTDOOR SPACE

Gay Search

Quadrille

Contents

Introduction

We live in an age of instant gratification. We can have what we want almost the moment we decide that we want it, whether it's a microwave meal or a takeaway, an online air ticket or the latest DVD from a website. Patience, it seems, is no longer a virtue.

The same is true when it comes to gardening. Many of us don't have time to garden, let alone wait for our garden to mature. We lead busy lives so we want to enjoy our gardens primarily by relaxing in them, not by slaving away. It's hardly surprising then that many of us are impatient landscapers too.

My *Little Book of Quick Fixes for Designing your Outdoor Space* is the answer. Its pages are packed with bite-size pieces of sound advice, tips and ideas that are accessible to even the most sceptical of impatient landscapers.

Throughout, you'll find the emphasis is on the impatient landscaper, with ideas that give you maximum drama for minimum effort. I even include my very own Impatient Landscaper's questions and answers!

Dip inside to find a host of easy, small-scale garden projects to do in a couple of hours – or a weekend at most – together with speedy garden fixes and planting ideas for instant results and long-term pleasure. And once you have the garden of your dreams, read my tips on how to keep it looking good all year long.

No matter whether your garden is cricket-pitch size or just a window box, you'll find my book is all you need to make your own private paradise – and in record time!

Gay Search

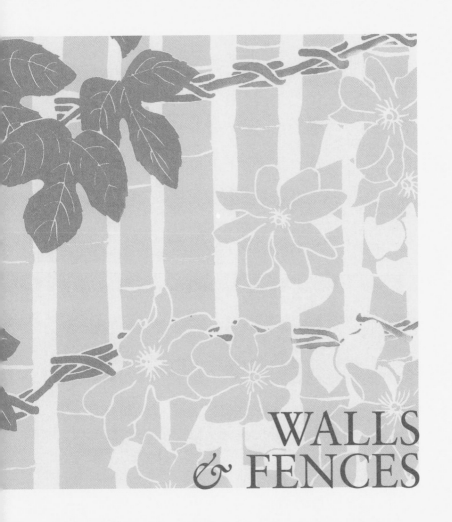

WALLS
& FENCES

Impatient Landscaper's
Questions

Q *Do I need a fence or wall around my garden, and if so, why?*

A Depending on where you live, you may not want a fence or wall around your front yard, or garden, but you probably need one around the back. In fact, these structures are a great asset to the impatient landscaper because they provide instant impact. In smaller gardens they are probably the most dominant element, especially in winter when there is little to distract from them. That's why it's essential to ensure that they are not merely functional but are worthwhile features in their own right.

Note that before erecting a fence or wall you should check with your local building codes for possible restrictions on height or materials.

Seven reasons why boundaries can be useful

1 They mark the extent of your property.

2 They provide shelter from the elements.

3 They create a warmer microclimate.

4 They provide some shade.

5 They provide an excellent backdrop to any planting scheme.

6 They provide privacy.

7 They can hide an unattractive view.

Did you know that...?

... densely planted walls or fences can make the boundaries of a garden disappear so that a lovely view, a nearby church spire, or even the trees in neighboring gardens appear to be part of your garden. The Japanese have a word for it—*shakkei*—meaning "borrowed scenery."

• • • whatever the size of your garden, internal divisions are useful because they enable you to create surprises and a sense of mystery. If the entire garden is laid out in front of you the moment you set foot in it, there's no motivation to explore, and it quickly becomes predictable and boring. But when there are divisions screening parts of the garden, you're lured out to discover what's around the other side.

Impatient Landscaper's Questions

Q *I've got a long, narrow garden. How can I stop it from feeling like a tunnel?*

A The worst thing is to have a path straight down the center and narrow borders on either side. This only emphasizes how narrow the garden is. If you divide the space up into a series of almost square, interconnecting "rooms," it makes the space appear wider than it actually is.

Different areas, different styles

Dividing your garden into a series of "areas," using screens or tall planting, gives you the opportunity to create different garden styles in these areas. Close to the house, for example, you could have a very formal paved area with a geometric pool and clipped box topiary in pots. Beyond the first screen, you could have a cottage garden, with soft, informal planting, or a Mediterranean gravel garden, or even a tropical garden. Beyond the next screen, you could have a wild area or a vegetable plot.

Screens make sense

Screens enable you to hide the less attractive elements in the garden—the toolshed, the compost pile, the trashcans.

Suit the planting to the boundary

♣ Attractive old brick walls call out for traditional planting—either romantic and informal, such as perennial borders or the cottage-garden look, or architectural and formal, as in parterres. Smooth, cement-faced surfaces or painted wood suggests more modern planting, with spiky architectural evergreens, grasses and perennials.

Suit the boundary to the garden

♣ Country gardens look best with informal screens such as mixed hedges—ideally, thorny ones to make them livestock-proof. Split-rail fences in various styles and, for a more enclosed effect, wattle or basket-weave fences complement country properties.

♣ City gardens need to reflect the built environment. There, the best-looking boundaries are walls, smooth-planed fences, cast-iron railings, or clipped formal hedges.

♣ For a front garden in small town, the traditional picket fence is a suitable option. One with scalloped upper edge (concave curves) would give a touch of elegance to both garden and house.

Impatient Landscaper's Questions

Q *I want to divide my garden up with some internal boundaries, but don't know what to use.*

A You don't have to worry about privacy or security where internal boundaries are concerned, so you have a wide choice. A living basket-weave fence, made of rooted saplings of willow or hawthorn, for example, makes an attractive instant barrier, offering, in summer, the bonus of their fresh green leaves. Plants also work—a group of shrubs, for example, or, in a small garden, even one very large specimen plant. Alternatively, a section of freestanding wall not only makes a dramatic division but also provides a strong sculptural element.

Did you know that...?

••• an internal boundary doesn't necessarily have to be vertical. A change of level will also send a message that you are in a different space. Crossing water has the same effect. A rill across the garden, perhaps with a stepping-stone or two, makes a very effective divide between different areas.

Two quick fixes for ugly walls

1 The easiest way to deal with ugly
walls is with masonry paint. It covers a
multitude of sins and brings unity to the
garden at a stroke. But if your walls are
in poor shape structurally, you should
have them re-pointed or even faced with
cement before you paint.

2 If the walls are beyond hope and you
can't afford to tackle them right away,
panels of marine plywood painted with
exterior-grade paint and nailed to the
walls offer an instant, low-cost, short-
term solution.

Color me beautiful

♣ When it comes to choosing color to paint your garden walls, consider the style of your garden carefully. Soft pastels—blues, greens, lavenders—are best in a traditional garden, while crisp neutrals—grays, stone, taupe— work well in a formal setting. Stronger shades, such as ocher, terracotta, and plum, are best in contemporary gardens. White is a good choice for a southern climate but in winter it can look rather harsh, especially in climates with lots of gray skies. Here, cream, soft yellow, or beige would be a better choice.

❀ Remember that color affects people's mood and will also affect the way you perceive the garden. "Hot" colors, such as red and orange, are stimulating and energizing, and will make a garden look smaller. "Cool" colors—blues and mauves—are relaxing and will make the space look bigger.

❀ You need to think, too, about the color as a backdrop for plants. Soft blues and greens work well with everything, while stronger tones look dramatic with a "hot" planting scheme.

Five instant tricks to liven up a dull wall

1 Use panels of trellis to break up a plain surface. They will give a 3-D effect and create attractive patterns of light and shade.

2 Parallel wooden battens of different lengths fixed to the wall also create interesting patterns and shadows. Paint them the same color as the wall for a subtle effect, or in a contrasting color for more drama.

3 Use stout galvanized wire to create geometric patterns—diamond shapes, zigzags, or fan shapes—on a plain surface. They add immediate interest; and in the longer term, you can grow small-leafed ivy along the wires, keeping it neatly clipped to keep the shapes sharp.

4 Get an artistic friend or relative to paint a
simple *trompe l'oeil* scene on the wall—or
paint one yourself—and place a window frame
over it. You'll create the illusion of looking out
onto another garden—or another place
entirely, such as a tropical beach.

5 Paint a dull brick wall with blue-green masonry
paint and hang a collection of galvanized metal
wall planters and watering cans on it.

Fence facelifts

The quickest and easiest way to make a
difference to existing fences is with color.
Choose from wood stain, through which
the grain of the wood will be visible, or
specially formulated paint for external
woodwork, which is opaque. Once upon
a time, wood stains came only in a range of
"natural" shades of brown or forest green,
but the choice of colors is much wider now,
with everything from subtle pastels
to bold brights.

Go organic

You can find organic wood stains made from natural ingredients such as beeswax and turpentine, or you can use pigments and Danish oil to make your own.

It's a cover-up

♣ The best quick-fix solution for mismatched fences is to cover them. The simplest option is to use bamboo—either sticks or whole canes—which you buy in a roll and fix to the fence posts. This look is really great for an oriental-style garden.

♣ For a contemporary garden, use plain panels of thin marine plywood fixed flush to the fence posts with metal brackets. You can then stain or paint the wood in the color of your choice.

♣ For a more formal, architectural look, fix beading to the panels before you paint. Glue it on with waterproof adhesive and hammer in a few panel pins for added security. The result looks like the molding on doors and cabinets.

Two-tone fences

You can use more than one color to paint your fences, but do so judiciously. For example, you could paint the posts and top rail in one color and the panels another or paint alternate slats in different colors to give the fence "rhythm." Lighter and darker tones of the same shade give a subtle effect, but use a contrast if you dare.

Oriental fantasy

Try using lacquer-red posts and black panels to make a fence in a Chinese-style courtyard garden.

Finishing touches

It's remarkable what a difference you can make simply by adding finials to your fence posts. Look for wooden balls, acorns, or pyramids to transform your purely utilitarian posts into architectural features in their own right.

Impatient Landscaper's Questions

Q *I'd like brick walls for my garden, but there are so many to choose from. Where do I start?*

A The best place to start is with your house. Ideally the bricks should match your house bricks as closely as possible. If you live in an older property, consider using secondhand bricks. They are not cheaper than new ones, but they have a lovely weathered quality and will blend with the house very quickly.

Concrete creations

Concrete is excellent for garden walls. It can be poured into a mold and colored, either with pigment mixed into the cement or by being painted with masonry paint after it has set. It can also be given texture by the wood used for the formwork.

The wave effect

Although boundary walls need to be straight, there is no reason why internal concrete walls can't be curved, or even wavy.

Three quick tricks for new fencing

1 For an attractive fence that gives privacy and good protection from wind, choose the "shadowbox" style. This consists of narrow vertical boards attached to alternated sides of the rails. Viewed head-on, it looks solid, but the narrow spaces created by the rail thickness permit some air circulation.

2 Cut the tops of your fence poles into points, like a stockade, or round them off for a softer, less aggressive, look.

3 Cut the fence poles all to the same length, or go for a wave formation or for castellations.

WESTCHESTER PUBLIC LIBRARY CHESTERTON, IN

Bamboo variety

Bamboo makes a light-looking boundary that works well in both rural and urban settings. Use either stout bamboo canes, palisade style; narrower canes, split and wired together and braced at the back for support; or even a grid of canes, trellis fashion, tied together with nonperishable twine or even with thin strips of leather tied in ornamental knots.

East meets west

Add interest to a small garden, without making it feel smaller, by dividing it with a screen of bamboo poles and rope.

FOR A 10-FOOT SCREEN

21 x bamboo poles approx. 4 inches in diameter

38 yards polypropylene rope that resembles hemp

21 x 1 x 1-inch pointed wooden stakes

2-foot long pieces of wood to act as wedges

1 Cut the bamboo poles to different lengths, ranging from 3 feet to 5 feet.

2 Hammer the pointed wooden stakes into the ground where you want each bamboo pole to be. Space them about the same distance apart as the diameter of the bamboo poles.

3 Break through the thin internal membrane of the bamboo at each nodule so that the bamboo will slide easily over the stake.

4 Slot a bamboo pole over each stake, arranging them to create a graceful curve at the top. They will wobble at first, but once they are tied together, they will be stable.

5 Wedge pieces of wood between the poles to keep them vertical and to maintain the correct tension as you tie the rope.

6 Link the poles at top and bottom with the rope, making a knot at each pole. The knots can be as simple or as ornate as you like.

7 Follow the curve of the screen with your rope and knots to achieve the best effect.

Solid support

For a town back garden, a solid board fence is a good option. You can choose to have the planks running either horizontally or vertically. Close-fitting hardwood planks laid horizontally have a contemporary feel and make the space feel wider. For a more informal look, leave the planks uneven. Vertical planks can be either slightly overlapping—"feathered"—or flush.

Contemporary choice

For a fence in a contemporary garden, try using square panels made from planks and placing them diagonally. These create a bold zigzag pattern along the boundaries. Since they are so strong visually, they work best in a rather minimalist setting. For the most stylish effect, use paint rather than stain.

Trellis works

Trellis works well in every style of garden.

* It is available in many patterns.

* It can look crisp and modern or warm and traditional.

* You can use stout trellis to make a useful screen within the garden, as well as on the boundary.

* It is especially good for small spaces because it doesn't close you in too much.

* Even before any plants start growing up it, trellis creates that all-important sense of privacy.

AT GROUND LEVEL

Impatient Landscaper's Questions

Q *How does what I put at ground level in my garden help me when I'm so impatient?*

A All garden floors are ideal for an impatient landscaper because they make a huge difference to the garden right away.

Impatient Landscaper's Questions

Q *Supposing I like a number of different ground-level treatments?*

A Most gardens have room for more than one type of surface, so you can have some variety. In a garden that is largely lawn and borders, there will be at least one terrace or patio, as well as paths, so you can move around the garden in all weathers. And in a city garden there may be room for some slabs or decking as well as some ground-cover planting.

Two reasons to choose hard landscaping instead of lawn

1 Small areas of lawn are not practical for family gardens because they take so much wear and tear that they never look good. The inevitable bare patches will end up muddy in winter and baked hard in summer.

2 If you have a lot of shade or large trees that suck all the moisture and nutrients out of the soil, a decent-looking lawn is simply not a realistic goal. Hard landscaping is the best alternative.

Did you know that…?

… a mixture of hard landscaping and planting is an attractive option. It's also practical because there will be areas you can use when a lawn would still be soggy after rain. And provided you choose plants that are easy to care for, it will be much less demanding in terms of maintenance than soft landscaping by itself.

Inside out

If your house opens out onto the garden, consider carrying the same material through to give the house and garden a sense of unity. Limestone, granite, slate, or large terracotta tiles are good options. Tiles will give the garden an instant Mediterranean feel—but make sure that you use frost-proof tiles outside.

All decked out

* Decking works very well in many situations, ranging from city backyards to rural locations.

* Decking blends well with garden planting.

* Decking can be cut to fit even the most awkwardly shaped areas.

* If left to weather, the wood becomes a lovely soft silvery gray and looks old and rustic.

* If it's color-stained, it has a smart contemporary appearance.

Impatient Landscaper's Questions

Q *My garden slopes away from the house, but I want somewhere to sit that's level. What are my options?*

A Decking is an excellent choice when you have big differences in level to contend with. In your kind of garden, it would be expensive and time consuming to terrace the site in order to create a flat area at the top for sitting out, but it's relatively straightforward to construct a wooden deck at the top of the garden. This can be supported on stout square posts and accessed by a flight of steps. With the addition of a simple balustrade for safety, the deck will provide not just a useful seating area but also a great view.

Impatient Landscaper's Questions

Q *I've got an old, cracked concrete patio and I want to cover it quickly. Any ideas?*

A Decking is a great choice to lay over existing surfaces. You don't have to dig out the concrete first, nor do you have to consider those boring but essential details such as the level of the house's waterproofing system. Since air circulates freely through and under decking, it doesn't matter if the decking finishes above the waterproofing.

Three decking choices

1 Hardwoods such as teak and oak are expensive but will last a lifetime. Pressure-treated softwoods are less expensive but can also last many years.

2 Consider using recycled lumber—old floorboards or even dismantled pallets. The aged appearance of old untreated floorboards is part of their charm; recycled pallets can be stained so that the wood is indistinguishable from new.

3 Choose between grooved and smooth decking. Some people think grooved decking is better, on the grounds that it is less slippery when wet, but in fact the grooves fill with soil and debris unless the decking is swept regularly, so you can end up with a smooth surface anyway. Ultimately it's a matter of personal choice.

A suitable case for treatment

Softwood that has not been pressure-treated needs to be specially treated to prolong its life. Either use a clear preservative every few years or colored wood stain, some types of which are specially formulated for decking.

Color effects

If you choose to use a wood stain on your decking, there is a good range of colors, from subtle silver grays to natural browns and more vibrant blues and yellows. But think carefully about your choice, because a large area of strongly colored flooring will have enormous visual impact, especially during the winter.

Impatient Landscaper's Questions

Q *Help! I've inherited an entire small garden made up of dirty, stained, concrete slabs. I don't want to keep them long term, but I can't afford to replace them right away. What can I do?*

A For a temporary improvement, use paint. It won't last indefinitely, but it will make a big difference. Start by cleaning the slabs with a proprietary patio and path cleaner or a pressure washer. Then paint them with masonry paint. Although it's not recommended for use on floors, it will last long enough to do the job you want it to do. It comes in a wide range of colors, so you can choose one to complement your garden's color scheme.

Impatient Landscaper's Questions

Q *I'd love to decorate my old slab floor with paint but I'm not very artistic. Is there anything I can do instead?*

A If you want only a small painted design, you could try using a stencil, either bought from a craft store or—if you're feeling adventurous—home made. Simple geometric shapes such as circles, ovals, and diamonds work best and are simple to use.

New life for tired slabs

A startling pattern of blue and orange circles can't fail to liven up an area of old slabs. Apply the design as a border or an allover random pattern. As a finishing touch, spray a simple terracotta bowl with copper acrylic all-surface aerosol paint and plant with several *Echeveria elegans*. These have fleshy blue leaves and tall slender sprays of bright orange flowers, which complement the paint colors very well. Echeverias are not hardy, so in winter bring them inside, where they make attractive houseplants.

YOU WILL NEED:
- stiff corrugated cardboard

- 1 can blue multisurface aerosol garden paint

- 1 can orange multisurface aerosol garden paint

1 Cut a piece of cardboard the same size as a slab. Cut a large circle out of the rectangle and a small circle out of the large circle.

2 Place the template in position on a slab and remove the large circle, leaving the small circle and the outer section in place.

3 Spray the slab using the blue paint.

4 When this is dry, replace the large circle, remove the small one and spray with orange paint.

5 Repeat as necessary.

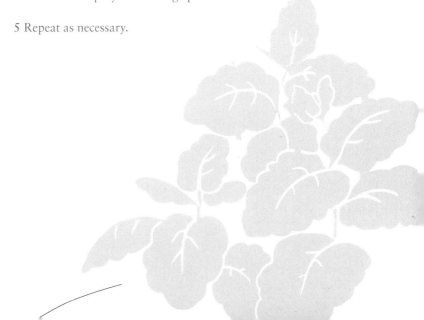

Patio paving facelifts

❀ Try replacing a few of your patio slabs—
perhaps some damaged ones, if there are
any—with a new, contrasting material, as in
the suggestions here.

❀ Use brick pavers laid in a herringbone pattern,
forming a series of "V"s, or in a basket-weave
design, with two pavers laid lengthwise, two
widthwise, and so on.

❀ Use old roofing tiles or slates. Cut them in
half and lay them side on in a zigzag or sun-
ray pattern.

♣ Try a mosaic made from small colored pebbles, or even seashells set in cement. Work out your pattern on paper first, and make sure the mosaic is flush with the surrounding paving by pressing lightly down on the mosaic with a plank as you work.

♣ Steel and brass washers in a variety of sizes look very stylish, especially if laid at random and overlapping.

♣ Use glass marbles or colored glass stones set in white cement, rather than the usual gray. This will give a light, bright background and show off the colors at their dazzling best.

Act natural

♣ If you're planning on a new floor surface for the garden, natural stone is superb. Whether it's old and weathered or newly cut, it comes in a beautifully subtle range of colors, from almost pure white to black, taking in everything including pinks, beiges, browns, purples, and grays en route. It is also extremely hardwearing and, unlike so many other materials, gets better with age.

♣ Slate, granite, sandstone, and carboniferous limestone (oölitic limestone is probably too soft for outside use) are all good choices. If you live in an area that has its own local stone, it makes sense to use it, not least because it will help keep costs down.

Impatient Landscaper's Questions

Q *I love the look of stone but can't afford it since the area I want to pave is pretty big. Is there an alternative?*

A Check out "reproduction natural stone." This is typically made of concrete and produced in molds imitating the texture of real stone, in some case quite convincingly. It comes in a range of colors; choose one that mimics the stone found in your region.

Color matters

❀ Before you commit yourself to a choice of stone slabs, look at them wet as well as dry, because the color can change quite dramatically—and in a rainy climate you'll be seeing them wet a lot of the time.

❀ It's also best to stick to one color. You may be tempted to indulge your creative urge and mix two or more colors of stone—perhaps in a checkerboard pattern—but the result could be an expensive mistake.

Dressed or undressed?

Dressed slabs have a smooth, sometimes almost polished, finish and perfectly straight edges, so they work best in formal or modern gardens. Undressed slabs, which have a riven, textured surface and irregular edges, work best in an informal setting. Here, use slabs of different sizes, and leave the edges unaligned and the joints unpointed. You could fill any gaps with soil mixed with seeds, such as Erigeron, Alyssum, or California poppies (*Eschscholzia*)—or wait for moss to colonize them.

Random thoughts

Irregular flagstones are a popular form of paving—not too expensive in parts of the country well supplied with stone. The stones can be laid with either soil or mortar joins. The first option allows you to insert fragrant plants, such as creeping thyme, between the stones; when trodden on, these release their scent, making the paved area even more attractive.

Size and scale

✿ One school of thought says that it's best to use the largest possible size of slabs in a small area, because that results in fewer joint. This will make the space look less "busy" and so it will feel larger. The other view is that where space is limited, very large units look out of proportion, and this will make the area appear even smaller, while more compact units, especially if laid in a simple, unfussy pattern, can make the space feel larger.

♣ Small units are easier to lay, because they need less cutting to make them fit. If you are doing the work yourself, base your layout on the dimensions of your materials to keep cutting to a minimum. Also, if your design involves curves or circles, small units are much easier to work with than larger ones.

Just add plants

You can add interest to an existing patio by removing some whole slabs and planting in the spaces. In a small patio though, large areas of planting can look out of proportion. In this case, remove just part of a slab.

Four evergreen carpeters to add interest to hard surfaces

1 Carpeting thymes are good value. They offer winter interest, have small pink, mauve, red, or white flowers in early summer, and release their fragrance when they are stepped on.

2 Thrift (*Armeria maritima*) is another good choice, forming soft hummocks of long, slender, bright evergreen leaves and producing masses of bright pink cloverlike flowers in summer.

3 The New Zealand burr (*Acaena microphylla* 'Copper Carpet' syn. *A. m.* 'Kupferteppich'), which forms a carpet of tiny coppery leaves with small, round, spiky flowers of chestnut brown, looks especially good with yellow bricks or sets.

4 *Stachys byzantina* 'Silver Carpet' is grown for its attractive furry silver leaves, not its flowers, so this nonflowering variety is particularly welcome. It makes an attractive ground-cover plant in very free-draining, gritty soil and full sun.

At Ground Level

A concrete idea

❧ Poured concrete is adored by many modern garden designers as a flooring material. It can be used to make any shape you like and can be tinted to produce a range of subtle or bold colors. It works best when it is unashamedly itself and not molded to mimic sets, cobbles, or pavers.

❧ Although any competent home handyperson or builder can lay concrete successfully, to exploit the design potential of the material fully, it is best to use a specialist company.

Go for brick...

♣ Match the bricks you use for garden paving as closely as possible to those of the house, though the house bricks themselves may not be ideal. Used on the ground, house bricks may absorb water, which expands as it freezes and contracts as it thaws. The result: Crumbly bricks. Instead, make sure you use frost-proof bricks.

❀ Brick comes in a number of different colors including a variety of shades of red and brown to deep yellow ocher and even cream.

...or try pavers

❀ Pavers, which have roughly the same visible dimensions as bricks when laid but are about half the thickness, are specially made for paving. There's a huge range of qualities and colors. Some are almost blue-black, which makes a striking contrast in a formal or modern garden.

A sense of direction

Laid lengthwise, bricks or pavers add
forward movement to a path or patio,
leading the eye off into the distance. Laid
widthwise, they draw the eye out to the
sides, emphasizing the width rather than
the length and so making the whole space
feel wider. Patterns such as basket weave
are static; in other words, they do not lead
the eye in any particular direction, and so
are more suitable for patios and other
sitting areas.

Get set

Sets are square (4-inch) blocks of granite, real or imitation, with a slightly rounded upper face. They are good for making intricate flooring patterns and for tight curves and circles. The curved tops give an interesting textured surface. Use them on their own, as decoration to break up an area of slabs or as an edging to contain gravel.

Six reasons to make gravel your choice

1 Gravel can have an informal or Mediterranean feel about it, or it can be formal, used with low clipped hedges to create a parterre effect.

2 It is an ideal material for integrating the hard and soft elements within a garden because you can grow plants through and even in it.

3 It's inexpensive.

4 It can be used for drives, parking areas, paths, and patios, as long as they have firm foundations.

5 It can be used to great effect in combination with other hard materials such as stone, bricks, and sets.

6 It can just be spread loose in borders to bring a uniform look to an area.

Did you know that...?

. . . gravel and stone chips are available in a wide range of colors, the colors varying depending on the area they come from. If you don't live in an area that produces its own gravel, choose a color range that blends with your house or with the other hard materials in the garden. Slate, for example, looks best with cool gray gravel, while yellow sandstone looks good with warm golden gravel.

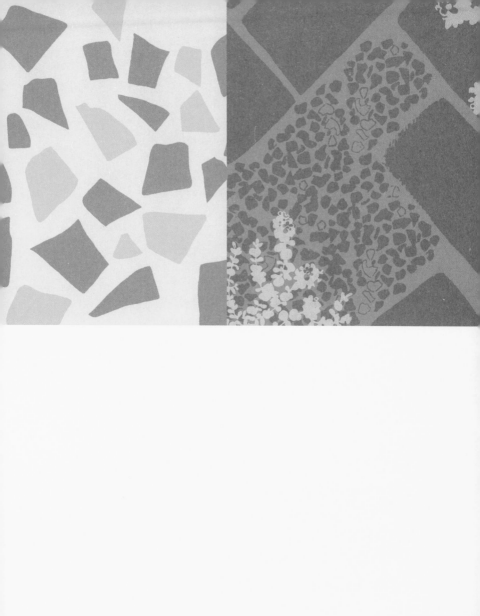

Size matters

* Gravel comes in different sizes, from very fine to chunky. A medium grade is most practical because it doesn't stick to your shoes and get walked into the house so easily. Also, cats find the stones too large and heavy to scratch in.

* If you are covering a slight slope, angular gravel is better than smooth, round pea gravel. The stones grip together and don't move as much.

Ouch!

For pedestrian traffic, gravel should be
at most 1 inch deep; otherwise it is
uncomfortable to walk on and will ridge
up. So either lay it on a firm foundation
or use a weed-suppressing membrane
underneath and stepping stones of another
material as a path through it.

Impatient Landscaper's Questions

Q *What will give me a similar look to gravel but with a more cutting-edge feel?*

A Crushed glass, which is laid in the same way as gravel, is a very stylish, though more expensive, option. It comes in a range of bright colors such as violet and turquoise. It has been tumbled to remove all sharp edges, so it is perfectly safe. Smooth, oval florists' beads are another option, but they are more expensive in large quantities.

Another very smart alternative is fine aluminum or stainless-steel chips or granules. You can even use crushed CDs.

Impatient Landscaper's Questions

Q *I like the look of these materials but don't want them to be distributed all over the garden by people or animals walking on them. Is there a solution?*

A Many of the finer grades can be bonded to a resinated base. This gives the same appearance but without the disadvantages.

Four reasons to choose grass

1 In the form of turf, which can be laid instantly like carpet, rather than seed, which takes some weeks to grow, grass is well suited to the needs of the impatient landscaper.

2 Grass works very well in traditional settings and there is no doubt that a sward of perfect emerald green sets plants off beautifully.

3 It's the obvious choice for medium and large gardens, both rural and urban, where hard landscaping would be both inappropriate and financially ruinous.

4 It's also the surface best suited to family gardens—provided the area of lawn is large enough—as it provides somewhere for children to play.

Turf special

- ♣ Living turf, or sod, looks good the instant it is laid—great for impatient landscapers—but a few weeks will elapse before it has rooted into the soil, is growing strongly, and can be walked on.

- ♣ Choose the grade of turf that is most suitable for the way you plan to use the lawn. Very fine grade looks best, though it needs a lot of upkeep. A tougher grade will take more punishment but won't look quite so plush. For a shady garden, choose a shade-tolerant grade.

✿ Turf is best laid when there is likely to be plenty of rain, so that the roots can become well established, and when the soil is neither too hot nor too cold. Depending on your climate, this might be in fall or in early spring; ask your local garden center for advice. If you choose to lay it in late spring or summer, make sure to keep it well watered, or the pieces may shrink, leaving ugly gaps between them.

Mowing made easy

Set stepping-stones or paving just below the level of the grass, so that the mower can skim over the whole area, removing the need for time-consuming edge trimming. Bricks or pavers can also form a useful barrier between lawn and border plants, which may be inclined to flop over it and kill off the grass underneath. If you like the look of irregular slabs of stone adjoining a lawn, be prepared to keep the edges trimmed with scissors!

The grass alternative

🍀 Chamomile and thyme are often suggested as alternatives to grass, but in large spaces they are a considerable amount of work in the early stages. In small areas, though, surrounded by hard materials, they are easier to maintain. Neither plant minds being trodden on occasionally; and indeed, when crushed, they release their fragrance. However, they would not make a suitable surface for family picnics or energetic games.

🍀 Corsican mint is another alternative, especially in shade. It has minute pale mauve flowers and very small round green leaves, which smell powerfully of peppermint when touched or walked on.

CONTAINERS

Two reasons to choose containers

1 If you have nothing more than a courtyard garden, balcony, roof terrace, or basement area, containers are your only option for growing plants.

2 If you have a proper garden, containers are a way of adding instant, eye-distracting beauty, either on a patio or sundeck or placed in a border among dull, neglected shrubs—perfect for impatient landscapers.

Impatient Landscaper's Questions

Q *I'm really short of time. Can I have containers that look good all year round without spending every weekend caring for them and replanting them?*

A Easy. You can plant a container for a display that lasts most of the year—bulbs for spring and bedding for summer and (climate permitting) winter. Choose small varieties of bulbs, so that once flowering is over, the dying foliage is not too prominent. Or you can grow plants for a short, spectacular season—regal lilies perhaps, for their breathtaking fragrance in midsummer, or a dazzling deciduous azalea in spring. Once they have finished their show, simply move them to a less prominent position, then bring them out again the following year.

Did you know that...?

... If you move often, containers are a good choice, because you can take them with you when you go.

You may be reluctant to spend a lot of money on a specimen tree to plant in the garden because you plan to stay only a year or two, but plant it in a suitably large container and you can take it with you. When you do finally settle down, simply plant the tree in the garden.

• • • containers are great for plants that may need some protection in winter. If there is no room for them inside over the winter, group them together in a sheltered corner of the garden and cover them with burlap or bubble wrap.

However, if you live in a cold climate, this may not be adequate; before buying a plant for a container, check its overwintering requirements with an expert at the garden center or nursery.

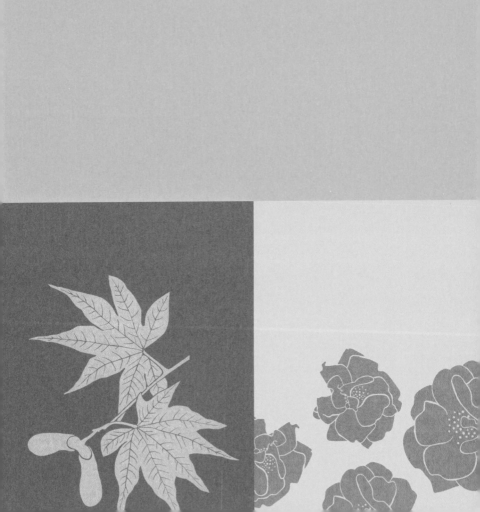

Impatient Landscaper's Questions

Q *I've never done any gardening before. What kind of plants can I grow in a container?*

A Almost anything, from a lettuce to a tree to a lettuce. Many small trees do well—for example, Japanese maples, magnolias, hollies, crab apples, and flowering cherry trees. You can also grow apples and cherries, as well as peaches and apricots. And that's not to mention a whole range of shrubs, particularly evergreens and roses—patio varieties, ground-cover, English roses, and climbing roses. Then there are perennials, such as hostas, ferns, and many grasses; also annuals and bulbs, especially the spring-flowering kind. The list is endless.

Just add water

You can even plant aquatic plants in your container. Use a large pot without a drainage hole, fill it between half and two-thirds full of soil or special aquatic soil mix, add a little carbon to prevent the soil from becoming sour and the water stagnant, then put in your plant. Finally, fill the pot with water. A pot like this is ideal if you go away a lot, because it can be left for several weeks without needing to be filled up with water.

Impatient Landscaper's Questions

Q *I've heard that some plants can be fussy about the soil they grow in. Is this true; and if so, what can I do if my garden's got the wrong kind of soil?*

A Go for containers. Some plants such as rhododendrons and camellias, need an acidic soil. If you do not have this in the garden, just plant them in containers. Equally, some Mediterranean plants, such as rosemary and lavender, hate heavy, boggy soil, so grow them in pots in a free-draining gritty planting mix.

Home grown

Edible crops such as herbs and salads—
especially cut-and-come-again salad
leaves—do well in containers; and small,
specially bred tomatoes can be grown
either in a pot or in a hanging basket,
along with some pale blue trailing
lobelia— an attractive and unusual
combination. Look for specially bred sweet
peppers, eggplants, and chilies for patio
containers, too.

Big is beautiful

Whatever container you choose, always go for the largest you can afford. Not only does one big one have greater impact than several smaller ones, but it is also more practical, because the soil mix will dry out less quickly and so need less watering.

Two designer tips

1 If you do want several containers, they
  will make more of a show if they are
  all the same style and material and are
  grouped together rather than dotted
  around.

2 If you have a large, particularly striking
  container, you could just leave it
  unplanted and have it make a strong
  sculptural statement among the planting
  in a border or on a patio.

What's inside?

* All containers need adequate drainage holes and a layer of drainage material to prevent the soil mix from washing into the holes. Traditionally "crocks"—broken pieces of terracotta flowerpot—have been used—but you can use large pebbles or broken slates or tiles. Where weight is a consideration, polystyrene packaging broken into manageable pieces is ideal.

* For permanent plantings, choose a rich, soil-based planting mix, while for temporary annual plantings, a soilless compost is fine. For permanent plantings on a roof or balcony where weight is a consideration, use a mixture of the two.

Material world

♣ There is a huge range of ceramic pots for the garden in all shapes and sizes, including Chinese cloud pots in rich dark blue or turquoise, hand-decorated pots from Latin American countries, dainty pots that look great as a table centerpiece, and wall-hanging pots with flat backs. Just make sure the pot's frost-proof before you buy.

♣ Wood, in the form of half-barrels or square rough-sawn tubs, suits informal, romantic gardens. Alternatively, for a formal setting, choose painted square Versailles tubs, with paneled sides and knobs at each corner.

♣ There are some very good wood imitation containers made of plastic or fiberglass that need little looking after. The best are made from molds of the genuine article, so the wood grain looks extremely convincing even close up.

♣ Square or rectangular lead tanks work well in a traditional setting, although the reproduction versions made from fiberglass are totally convincing, are much lighter in weight, and carry no health risk. Other metals, such as copper, aluminum, stainless steel, and galvanized metal in strong, simple geometric shapes, look very good in a modern formal garden.

♣ Glass containers need to be thick and toughened. Try them for growing plants such as the tall papyrus (*Cyperus papyrus*) hydroponically, in layers of colored gravel or bright plastic chips and water. If you want to grow plants in the normal way in glass, you will need drainage holes in the bottom of the container—get a professional to make them for you.

❀ Baskets woven from willow make terrific
containers if you treat them with several coats
of colored wood stain or waterproof marine
varnish first and line them with sturdy black
plastic sheets before you plant. They will not
last forever but will give you a lot of container
for your money for a few years.

❀ Large stone urns look marvelous in large
gardens—evoking the great classical gardens
of Italy and France—but they can also be
stunning in very small city gardens, where
their disproportionate scale is very dramatic
and exciting.

♣ Genuine antique stone containers can cost as much as a secondhand car, but reproduction urns of reconstituted stone are cheaper, and concrete replicas are cheapest of all. These do look rather stark and new but can easily be "distressed" with a hammer and chisel, and a coat of well-watered-down dark brown latex paint to age them. If you can curb your impatience just this once, try this relatively quick "fix": paint them with plain yogurt or sour milk, or even liquid manure. This quickly encourages algae and lichen to grow on them, adding a welcome patina of age.

Terracotta tradition

♣ Terracotta containers work well in almost all gardens but are particularly good in an informal or romantic setting. They are available in a range of styles, from plain machine-made flowerpots to highly decorated hand-thrown pots. Your choice will be dictated by taste and budget; but, especially if you are buying expensive terracotta, make sure it is guaranteed frost-proof.

♣ A row of terracotta half pots filled with lavender have a soft, traditional feel while still looking formal.

Not quite terracotta

🍀 Very good plastic imitation terracotta pots look almost like the real thing. They have the advantage of being lightweight and unbreakable, although they do not age in the same way.

🍀 They can look extremely stylish with a paint effect. Try an easy-to-use kit for a verdigris, pewter, or rusty-iron look. Always use an acrylic undercoat and seal with waterproof varnish.

Simple or ornate?

The more elaborate the container, the simpler the display of plants in it needs to be, and vice versa. So a very ornately decorated pot will look stunning with just one type of plant—for instance, trailing scarlet pelargoniums or blue-leafed hostas—while a plain wooden half-barrel needs a more interesting combination of shapes and colors.

Pack them in

The most attractive containers are those that are packed with plants. You don't want to see any bare potting mix; and, in the case of a simple container, you don't want to see a great deal of the container, either.

Ups and downs

Choose plants of different habits—some trailing to soften the edges, some upright to add height to the display, and some bushy to fill in.

Impatient Landscaper's Questions

Q *I haven't got a clue about color schemes for my container planting. Can you help?*

A A limited range of colors works best. A combination of red, white, and blue is always popular with traditional landscapers, while for a romantic garden, pastels such as pink, mauve, and pale blue, as well as white, together with silver foliage look terrific. Single-color planting can look stunning, too. Yellow, for example, ranges from deep cream through lemon, butter, and apricot to deep gold. White is always very elegant. Here the interest comes from the contrasting flower shapes and sizes, together with the different greens of the foliage. Try tiny white lobelia or baby's breath, with larger impatiens and big blowsy double begonias.

Perfect positioning

In a formal garden, part of what makes the difference to your containers is where you position them. A pair of identical containers to either side of a front door or a bench, for example, immediately adds a sense of formality; or try four matching containers at the corners of a square or rectangular pool.

Did you know that...?

... architectural plants—those with very large, boldly shaped leaves—are ideally suited to formality because they reinforce the simple geometry of the containers themselves. Spiky evergreen cordylines, phormiums, and large-leafed hostas are all very good choices.

Two topiary tales

1 Topiary—small-leafed evergreen shrubs, such as box, euonymus, or holly, clipped into geometric shapes—is an excellent choice for container planting. All an impatient landscaper needs is a single box ball or lollipop, spiral, or pyramid to make an immediate impact.

2 Box topiary takes careful training over a number of years, so it's an expensive buy. As a less expensive alternative, stand a trellis or wire obelisk in your container. This will create that sharp architectural outline right away, then you can grow a fast-growing plant such as a small-leafed, English ivy over it. If you keep it well clipped, the outline will remain crisp and the angles sharp.

Herbal checkerboard

This herb garden is perfect for the impatient landscaper who also loves to cook, because it can be used—judiciously—from Day One. Your choice of herbs depends on what you most like to use and what will suit the conditions best. For example, mint likes some shade, whereas Mediterranean herbs, such as thyme and rosemary, need sun. And since this herb garden should be decorative as well as functional, choose herbs that look, as well as taste, good.

YOU WILL NEED

5 square metal containers,
12 x 12 x 12 inches

approximately 15 feet
of 2 x 1-inch lumber

4 "L" brackets

black gloss paint for exterior use

1 x 2-quart pot
Rosmarinus 'Miss Jessopp's Upright'

4 x 3½-inch pots *Salvia officinalis* 'Purpurascens'

4 x 3½-inch pots mint

4 x 3½-inch pots chives

4 x 3½-inch pots *Foeniculum vulgare* 'Purpureum'

soil mix

decorative mulch of crushed CDs, or fine gravel

1 Arrange the 5 metal containers in a checkerboard pattern.

2 Make a frame of 2- x 1-inch lumber, joined at the corners with simple metal "L" brackets and large enough to surround the containers.

3 Paint the frame black, and put it in position.

4 Fill the containers almost to the top with the soil mix and plant one with rosemary, one with purple sage, one with mint, one with chives, and one with bronze fennel—or with herbs of your own choice.

LIGHTING

Impatient Landscaper's Questions

Q *I may be an impatient landscaper, but I'm not a millionaire. Why on earth should I bother with any garden lighting? Isn't it just another unnecessary expense?*

A There are so many advantages to garden lighting, it's difficult to know where to begin. For a start, it enables you to enjoy all the other features in your garden, whether you are sitting outside or looking at the garden from indoors. And if you go out to work, you probably have little opportunity to enjoy your garden because it's so often dark by the time you get home. The use of lighting can change all that.

In fact, your garden may look even better at night, because you can highlight the very best parts and hide the less attractive ones under a forgiving cloak of darkness—especially important if you are an impatient landscaper who has improved only one area of the garden so far.

And finally, since you're so impatient, remember that lighting gives you instant drama at the flick of a switch.

Did you know that...?

... lighting can be as simple or as complicated as you like. Choose from simple candles or lanterns or go for electric lights—either low-voltage systems you can install yourself or more sophisticated lighting that needs to be installed by a professional.

The simplest of simple lighting effects for a special occasion

✿ Drape strings of low-voltage outdoor lights over the branches of trees or shrubs or over statues or obelisks. Choose from little round pea lights, light-emitting diodes (LEDs) in flexible plastic tubing, or fiber-optic cables. Colored lights are fun for a party. Set them to twinkle or "chase" each other. Most of these lighting sets come with a programmer and a number of programming options.

✿ Hang glass and metal lanterns with votive lights inside from the branches of trees or big shrubs or put glass hurricane lamps on a garden table.

* Use a mass of glass jars with a tealight in each to light a path, along the top of a wall, or in a large group on the patio floor. The more you have, the more magical the effect. If you want some color, simply paint the outside of the jars with translucent glass paint.

* Make some luminarias: Part-fill larg,e stiff brown paper bags with sand for stability and add a tealight to each. They will cast a lovely warm golden glow. You can buy bags that have been specially treated with a fire-retardant.

* If you have a pool or pond, float some special floating candles in it. The slightest movement of the water makes both the real and the reflected flames dance and sparkle.

* Candles pushed into the soil in flowerpots are an instant and very inexpensive form of garden lighting.

Impatient Landscaper's
Questions

Q *Must I have a professional to install my garden lighting?*

A While you can install some low-voltage do-it-yourself lighting, you will need a qualified electrician for most kinds of lighting, especially lighting associated with water. And since lighting your garden is not just about the practicalities but about aesthetics, too, it is worth employing a professional to design the layout.
A good designer will arrive at your home with a set of lights to show you how the garden could look at night.

But whichever approach you choose, if you are planning a garden from scratch, think about the lighting from the start, rather than adding it as an afterthought once the garden is finished.

Degrees of separation

If you want to install sensor-triggered security lighting, it needs to be on a separate circuit.

A touch of theater

Take your cue from theater lighting to achieve the best lighting effects in your garden.

🍀 *Front light*

Statues and particularly ornate urns or pots are best lit from the front, so that the detail is revealed. If they are lit from behind, you tend to just see a silhouette.

🍀 *Side light*

Side lighting is best for an object whose three-dimensional shape is its outstanding feature, such as a simple pot or an abstract sculpture.

Side lighting is ideal for illuminating steps or other changes of level.

❀ Bottom light

Trees look fantastic lit from below, their tracery of branches standing out against the darkness.

Lighting from below with uplighters is great for walls, too. Around an eating area they create a soft background glow. You could also add a few candles on the table so people can see what they're eating.

Uplighters can be used to mark a path if you're looking for a subtle effect.

❀ Top light

Downlighters create discrete pools of light, which is another useful way of marking features such as steps. You can either hang the fixtures low enough for them to be hidden by any planting or suspend them high up in a tree, where they can shine down through the branches.

What's your style?

You can use light to emphasize the style of your garden. In a formal garden, for example, narrow beams of light at regular intervals shining up a wall would add to the formality, whereas softer more diffuse lights, set at different angles and washing over the wall, would give a much more informal feel. In modern gardens, the latest technology in fiber optics, as well as neon, takes lighting into the realm of art.

Water wizardry do's and don'ts

✿ Do use uplighters underwater in a formal pool. They look especially good placed directly under a fountain or jet.

✿ Do try an underwater uplighter in a simple bubble fountain. It will steal the show.

✿ Do turn the spotlight on a wall fountain and watch each falling droplet sparkle in the light.

✿ Do try side lighting for a pool. It creates strong shadows from any planting and turns a still surface into a mirror, giving you great reflections.

✿ Don't use downlighters in a pond because they reveal all the mechanics—cables, pumps, pond liners—and of course, any debris in the water. They also create an uncomfortable glare.

Shadow play

When you're planning your lighting effects, you also need to consider the impact that shadow has. An architectural plant lit from below will cast fantastic magnified shadows on a nearby wall. In my own garden, the shadows cast by the jagged blue leaves of *Melianthus major* look like palm trees on my terracotta wall and turn a part of southwest London at night into southern California.

ARCHES
& ARBORS

Impatient Landscaper's Questions

Q *What's the difference between an arbor, a pergola, and a gazebo?*

A Traditionally, an arbor was a leafy bower of densely planted trees or shrubs trained together overhead to create a private, shady place to sit. Now, the term is more widely used for any enclosed seating area where plants, though still important, no longer form the structure.

A pergola consists of a series of uprights linked by overheads. It's rather like a walk-through "tunnel," so you often find one standing on a path. It can also be attached to the house, making a useful visual link between house and garden.

Gazebos were primarily ornamental, adding structure to the garden or framing a statue. They are usually round or octagonal in shape, so they need to be in an open, prominent position.

Three ways of using arches

1 A simple arch divides the garden and so creates a sense of surprise, which is especially important in a small garden, where the tendency is to see the whole garden the moment you step out into it.

2 Position an arch in front of a wall, grow some lovely climbers over it, place a seat underneath, and presto! you've got a leafy arbor.

3 Line up two or three arches and you've got a pergola.

Did you know that...?

... pergolas, arches, and arbors not only add height and structure to your garden but also are important to the way you use and enjoy the space, giving you a sense of being inside even though you are outside. And they also help create a feeling of privacy, which, in overcrowded cities with neighbors so close by, is invaluable.

All in the mind

* Although you can have an arbor that is completely enclosed with solid wood or trellis, even a light structure of poles, ropes, or netting creates a haven and makes you feel safe from prying eyes.

* Enclosing part of your garden with a pergola makes the spaces at each end feel more open and therefore larger.

* Pergolas can suggest movement around the garden—dividing it up and yet linking different areas.

Eight pergola pointers

1 Stone or brick piers with wooden overheads were popular in nineteenth- and early twentieth-century gardens, but wood is the most common choice for the uprights these days, since it is relatively inexpensive and quick to erect.

2 For a modern garden, try using an "industrial" material such as scaffolding poles, welded square-section metal, or steel I beams painted with tough external-grade enamel. Lengths of copper piping or stainless-steel chain or cable can make a striking overhead for a wooden pergola.

3 For a more organic look, make the overheads from stout twisted polypropylene rope that looks like hemp, or from lengths of bamboo.

4 In an informal garden, and especially at some distance from the house, natural-looking rustic poles have a cottage-garden feel; but close to the house, and certainly in more formal gardens, square posts are better. You can make them look even smarter by chamfering the corners and painting or staining them either a dark color—navy or black—or a pale blue-green or gray.

5 Square, unpainted wooden overheads give a solid, chunky feel, whereas narrower beams, arranged in a grid, are more elegant, especially if the ends of the beams are shaped.

6 If you've got the space, consider positioning a pergola at a point where two paths cross.

7 In a very small garden, it's best to attach a pergola to the house or to a side wall, rather than have it freestanding, where it will take up a lot of space.

8 Your pergola—or any garden arch, for that matter—must be tall and wide enough for people to walk under and through, even when it is clothed with plants.

Did you know that...?

... an arbor is perfect for the impatient landscaper, because it's very striking visually and has instant impact.

An open and shut case

✿ Some arbors are made of solid wood, somewhat like sentry boxes. They can be rectangular or arched, plain or fancy, double or single; and some have a built-in seat.

✿ Other arbors are made from trellis panels, with the degree of enclosure they offer depending on the spaces between the battens.

Traditional...?

Woven willow or hazel makes an attractive arbor. Hazel works better in an informal garden, because it's somewhat chunkier-looking, while willow makes very clean shapes, which are good in a formal setting. You can leave the twigs unpainted or give them a wash of color—pale gray or even white looks very stylish.

...or modern?

Unashamedly modern materials, such as polycarbonate panels, especially used in conjunction with steel uprights, make a striking contemporary arbor. It will be well sheltered from the wind, private, and yet filled with light.

Tasteful toolsheds

Toolsheds are functional, but that doesn't mean they have to be ugly. Instead of hiding them behind a screen, paint them an attractive color to make a statement—beach-umbrealla blue-and-white stripes in a gravel garden, for example, or rich dark green with brass hardware.

Gazebo glamour

❀ Gazebos may sound rather grand, but it is possible to find them at a size and price suitable for most gardens; and they not only add weight to the overall design of the garden but also provide a sheltered place to sit, even on days that are bright but chilly.

❀ If you want your gazebo to blend in, paint it the same color or perhaps a shade darker or lighter than the surrounding greenery or boundaries. If you want to make it a focal point, use a contrasting shade.

FURNITURE

Impatient Landscaper's Questions

Q *What's the quickest—and cheapest—thing I can do to stop my overgrown garden from looking neglected?*

A Just buy a good-looking garden chair—even a simple, colored, plastic folding chair will do—and pop it in the garden in a spot that catches the sun. It will make an instant focal point, no one will notice the wildness around it, and you'll have somewhere great to sit as well.

Shopping advisor

♣ Seats must be comfortable and tables sturdy.

♣ Tables and chairs must be easily moved and stored if they are not weatherproof.

♣ In very small gardens, particularly, tables and chairs have to look good because they will be a very prominent part of the scene.

♣ If you want wooden furniture, choose from hard- or softwood. Hardwood can stay outside in winter and will last for many years. If you oil it regularly, it will keep its glossy brown color; otherwise it will weather to a silvery gray. Pressure-treated softwood is less expensive and won't last quite as long, though regular treatment with colored wood stain or opaque paint will prolong its life.

♣ Curved wood furniture is expensive because the curves are achieved by complicated lamination and steaming.

♣ Reproduction cast-aluminum tables and chairs are lightweight and don't need much maintenance.

♣ Seats molded from polypropylene resin in bold free-form shapes and bright colors are surprisingly comfortable and very sculptural when not in use.

♣ Plastic garden furniture is the cheapest. If that's all your budget allows, you can brighten it up by treating it with an acrylic undercoat and spraying it an interesting color with spray paint formulated for plastic.

One style suits all

Simple café-style tables and chairs work in almost every style of garden. Plain aluminum or bright, funky lime green, orange, or blue makes a youthful statement. Off-white, pastels, and dark green have a more classic appeal.

In with the new

Wooden furniture for modern gardens should have simple clean lines, whether angular or curved.

In with the old

Traditional Mission Style or Chinese Chippendale benches work well with tables and chairs in strong geometric shapes.

Old to new

A random collection of old kitchen chairs takes on a more unified look when painted all the same color or in complementary shades. They won't be weatherproof, though, so remember not to leave them out in the garden.

Sun worshiper

Look for the corner of the garden that catches the last rays of the sun, and put some seating there.

Spaced out

If storage space is a problem, buy folding
garden chairs in bright colors and hang
them on the garden walls. Instant art!

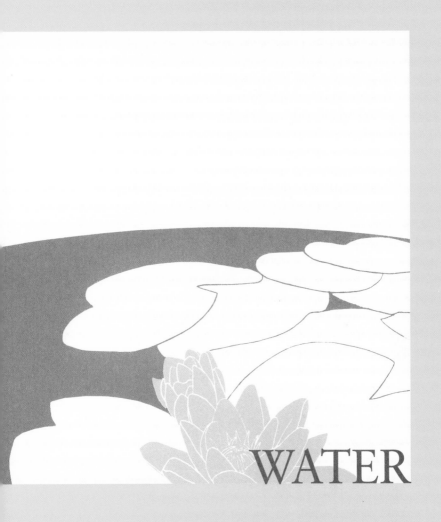

WATER

Three good reasons to have a water feature in the garden

1 It brings a sense of movement to the garden. Even a still water feature does this in the form of ripples across the surface and reflections of clouds and of plants moving in the wind.

2 The sound of water is wonderfully relaxing, especially in busy towns and cities.

3 Water attracts a whole range of wildlife—birds, frogs, dragonflies—often within days, if not hours.

Impatient Landscaper's
Questions

Q *I'm an impatient landscaper looking for a quick fix. A water feature doesn't sound very quick to me.*

A That's where you're wrong. You could make a barrel pond on the patio in no time at all. Put a layer of gravel or pebbles in the bottom of a watertight wooden barrel, add a couple of aquatic plants in their plastic baskets plus a bunch of oxygenating weed, and fill with water. Just make sure the barrel is at least 12 inches deep. Also make sure that local building codes do not prohibit standing water in your area, as is often the case where mosquitoes are a problem.

Even simpler, fill a large shallow bowl with
water, add a few iridescent glass stones for some
sparkle, and stand it in a sunny position
on your patio.

Or if you're a bird lover, just add a birdbath
to the garden, sit back, and enjoy.

For moving water, though, you'll have to have
an outdoor electricity supply on a separate
circuit—and for that you'll have to call on the
services of a professional electrician. Check your
local building codes for requirements on
installing wiring for water features.

Pool your ideas

❀ In an informal garden go for a natural-looking pool. You can buy pre-formed fiberglass liners, but they give an unnatural shape. Far better to use a flexible pond liner and give your pond generous free-flowing curves rather than lots of fussy ins and outs.

❀ Dense planting helps to blur the edges of the pool and make it blend in with its surroundings in a naturalistic way.

❀ If you plan to keep fish, your pool must be at least 24 inches deep so the fish are safe from predatory birds and from ice if the water freezes in winter.

* A shelf around the side of the pool about 12 inches down enables you to grow attractive marginal plants in baskets, as well as deep-water plants and oxygenators to keep the water healthy.

* A formal pool should be a strong geometric shape—square, rectangular, or circular. The geometry is important in a formal setting, so it's best to leave the pool unplanted. This will give the best reflective quality to the water, too. To enhance this, either use a black pond liner or have the inside of the pool faced with cement and painted with black pond paint.

Big and bold

Be bold with pools, and make them as large as possible. The impact they make is so much greater; and, besides, large pools are easier to maintain than small ones.

Impatient Landscaper's Questions

Q *I've had the wiring done, but before I buy a pump, what sort of water-feature options are there for me to consider?*

A There's lots of choice, depending on your taste and budget. You can buy a ready-made water feature, such as an old-fashioned hand pump pouring water into a barrel, which is fun in a country-style garden, or a wall fountain, which suits a formal garden.

You could install a bubble fountain. Dig a hole for the reservoir and pump. Once they're in place, cover the lid of the reservoir with pebbles, stone chips, crushed glass, or florists' glass stones, turn on the power and you're off and running.

Or you could install a large metal or glass sphere over a reservoir. The sphere is hollow, and when the water is pumped up through it, surface tension makes the water cling to the sides. The surface of the sphere comes alive with the subtle movement of the water catching the light.

Three ideas to keep you on the level

1 Try rills or channels, no more than 10 inches wide or deep, dissecting the garden. This idea originated thousands of years ago in Persian "paradise gardens." The Persians believed that the universe was divided into four quarters, so the earliest paradise gardens were divided into four by rills. Your rills could run parallel or could intersect. Each would need its own reservoir and pump to keep the water flowing.

2 Make a much broader rill and fill it with rows of widely spaced sets so the water flows between them. Although it would look as though you were walking on water, in fact your feet would remain dry.

3 In a modern garden, try small oblong or cross-shaped pools set into smooth concrete or resinated aggregate and lined with aluminum. The effect is stunning.

Chuting star

A stainless-steel chute or a steel I beam set in a smooth concrete wall, pouring a sheet of water into a slender rectangular pool looks very striking in a contemporary setting.

FEATURES

Did you know that...?

... features are the finishing touches that give a garden personality. More than anything else, they can stamp your personality on the garden, distill its essence, and create a mood. For the impatient landscaper, they are ideal, because all that is required in most cases is a bit of careful thought about where to place them to best advantage.

Don't break the bank

The type of feature you choose depends not only on the style of your garden but on your bank balance. Antique stone classical figures are very expensive—too expensive to risk leaving outside—but there are good-quality reproductions available, which make very acceptable alternatives. There are also less expensive, slightly rougher concrete versions, made from molds. These would work well in a less formal setting, especially after a bit of "distressing" (see page 143) and if you position them among the plants.

Impatient Landscaper's
Questions

Q *I love antique stone, and think it would suit my garden style, but I've had a look and don't think my purse will stretch to a big piece like a statue. Apart from reproduction stone, are there any other alternatives?*

A If you're determined to have a piece of antique stone, investigate architectural salvage yards for ornate finials, broken pediments, chunks of column, or even pieces of statue—a severed head or maybe a pair of feet. These can look very good, especially if you stand them on a plinth.

Infinite variety

Garden features, whatever they're
made of, change according to the light at
different times of day and different times
of year. They will also be a different
color when wet or dry, and if they are
placed among plants, will assume more or
less prominence according to the season.

Pure abstraction

Abstract sculpture can work well in any style of garden, depending on the material and how the piece is displayed. A beautiful, smooth, crafted metal, wood, or stone piece displayed on a simple plinth would work equally well in a traditional formal garden or a modern one. A more free-form, angular, or organic piece would be better in an informal or modern setting.

Animal farm

Animal sculptures—bronze geese, chicken-wire sheep, even rusting metal hippos—can also work well, but they must be aesthetically pleasing in their own right and/or great fun. You may think rabbits pushing wheelbarrows, porcupines on their hind legs, or "mooning" gnomes fall into this category. No comment.

Special commission

If you can't find exactly the sort of
feature you want, contact a local sculptor—
perhaps through a local art school—and
commission a piece. It need not be
prohibitively expensive unless the sculptor is
famous. You'll end up with something that
suits both your personality and your garden.

Formal...

🍀 In a formal garden, a sculpture looks best against a simple background such as a hedge or a wall covered in evergreen climbers. That way, its contours stand out very clearly.

🍀 Placing any sculptural object on a plinth immediately gives it a much more formal, thought-out look.

...meets informal...

🍀 In a more informal setting, sculpture is most effective among planting, where its solidity and artifice contrast beautifully with the foliage around it. In Vita Sackville-West's famous white garden at Sissinghurst, in Kent, for example, a pale gray lead statue of a vestal virgin stands under the canopy of a silver weeping pear.

* Placing a sculptural object on the ground produces an informal effect—and adds an element of surprise.

...somewhere between

* Natural materials such as pieces of driftwood, bleached and worn by the sea, look fantastic in a natural setting, where they appear to be part of the landscape. But put them in a formal or modern setting and the contrast between nature and artifice has an even more powerful effect.

Rock on

* Jagged pieces of rock work very well in an oriental-style or modern garden. Place them on a patio or in a gravel garden, either lying flat or standing upright, reminiscent of Stonehenge.

* Large, smooth boulders are effective too, either on hard landscaping, to contrast with the geometry of the paving, or among planting, where their contours enhance the shapes and texture of the leaves.

Six garden features to go

1 A group of tall stainless-steel spirals—sold as tomato supports—can look stunning in a modern setting.

2 Solar panels move in the wind and can be wired to a battery to provide power to operate a water feature or some garden lighting, thereby adding function to form.

3 Old horticultural and agricultural implements are worth looking for. Many, though, such as old millstones, plows or watering cans, now have antique status and a price tag to match.

4 Industrial machine parts are often surprisingly beautiful. Old grinding wheels or cogs look strikingly architectural on top of a wall, whether an old brick wall or a modern concrete one.

5 Ball bearings come in a range of sizes, up to 36 inches in diameter. These make perfect stainless-steel spheres to stand on the paving in a minimalist garden.

6 Old CDs make great mobiles, hanging from trees and sending shafts of light darting all around the garden. They are also good for keeping the birds off edible crops, so they are functional, too.

PLANT MAGIC

Can't wait, won't wait?

* If you're an impatient landscaper, you want to start getting pleasure from your garden right away, whatever the time of year; so get planting and be bold.

* For maximum drama, use loads of the same plant and put them all together—fifty narcissuses in a huge clump look far better than ten dotted all around.

* For maximum impact, stick to one or, at most, two colors.

* For maximum enjoyment, plant in a spot that you can see from the house—from the kitchen or dining window, or through the patio doors.

* If it's winter, plant in containers a variegated holly, perhaps. Ask an expert at your local garden center what works well in your climate.

* In summer make the most of annuals—and add some height with a forest of tall sunflowers or a mass of beautiful, scented *Nicotiana sylvestris*.

* While you're waiting for your hardy annuals to flower, place a large pot among them, planted with bright spring bedding—forget-me-nots, pink and white daisies (*Bellis*), or some wallflowers.

Lasting pleasure, minimal effort

Here's a sizzling purple and yellow planting idea that will give you a burst of color in early spring (maybe even earlier) and well into the summer.

* In the fall, clear an area at least 24 x 12 inches. Plant a minimum of a dozen mid-season yellow tulips per 12 inch square, each tulip evenly spaced, not touching the next and in a hole at least three times its own depth. Fill in around the bulbs with soil, then plant a mixture of purple pansies and blue forget-me-nots on top. Don't worry the tulips—they'll find space to push up through.

* Depending on your climate and on the variety of pansies you choose, you may get blooms during the winter, provided they get some sunlight. By early spring, flowering should be well under way, followed soon by the tulips and forget-me-nots.

Climbers

Grown up obelisks or tepees, climbers can give height far more quickly than any other plants, and they can brighten up walls and fences, too. They are also invaluable for adding interest to existing shrubs or hedges that are serviceable but dull. These will give a good show even in the first year that you plant them.

In the following plant portraits, ☆ is used to show a Temporary Star, a plant that can be removed once surrounding plants have reached a decent size. ◯ is used to show a Stayer, a plant to enjoy for many years.

Clematis armandii

SIZE AFTER ONE SEASON:
6 x 6 feet

ULTIMATE SIZE:
25 x 25 feet

ZONES
7—9

This evergreen clematis is a handsome plant for a town garden, producing long, slender, leathery leaves and masses of white (*C. a.* 'Snowdrift') or blush white (*C. a.* 'Apple Blossom') flowers in spring, which are also scented. It is good trained up and along the top of a wall or allowed to scramble through an old tree. Although it is hardy down to 5°F, it does best with some protection from cold winds. Like all clematis, it is happiest with its head in the sun and its roots in the shade. It tolerates both acid and alkaline soil, but prefers it to be well drained but moisture-retentive. It climbs by means of tendrils, so give it something to latch onto such as a grid of wire. It needs no pruning unless it outgrows its allotted space, though some older stems can be shortened to encourage more vigorous new growth.

Passiflora caerulea
Blue passion flower

**SIZE AFTER
ONE SEASON:**
6 x 6 feet

ULTIMATE SIZE:
20 x 20 feet

ZONES:
7—10

This is a vigorous climber with attractive hand-shaped leaves and curious white, purple, and blue flowers from midsummer to fall. It also has fruit in late summer and fall. It is a rambler and is best trained over wires or trellis. It loses its leaves in winter, and the top growth can be killed off in very cold weather, but in most cases it will produce new growth in the spring. Where space is confined, it can be cut hard back to within 3 feet or so of ground level in early spring and will quickly regrow. It does best in full sun but can tolerate light shade, and can cope with all soil types except very dry or very alkaline ones.

Polygonum aubertii
Silver-lace vine

SIZE AFTER ONE SEASON:
9 x 9 feet

ULTIMATE SIZE:
20 x 20 feet

ZONES:
4—7

The perfect plant for the impatient landscaper, silver-lace vine grows with a wild abandon that belies its ladylike name. Plant a seedling by a fence or an arbor, and within a couple of seasons it will have completely covered the structure. The deciduous glossy, bright green foliage is followed in midsummer, and well into fall, by a profusion of delicate creamy white flowers, borne in long panicles. Silver-lace vine will thrive in cold winters (down to -30 degrees F) and long dry spells. However, you must be prepared to prune it severely to keep it from taking over your garden!

Three quick fixes for a shady side passageway

1 For an informal look, paint the walls or fences
   a very pale color, and freshen up the floor with
   masonry paint, pale stone chips, or pale gray
   decking. Add trellis to the walls and hang pots
   of ferns, fuchsias, lobelia, or tuberous begonias
   from it. Along the base of the wall, use deep
   troughs planted with hostas and more ferns;
   and if you want climbers, choose a brightly
   variegated evergreen ivy such as *Hedera helix*
   'Oro di Bogliasco' (syn. *H. h.* 'Goldheart') or
   H. h. 'Glacier'.

2 For a formal look, decorate with evergreen box balls, lollipops, or spirals in square tubs or simple terracotta pots. Add a few pots of hostas, or alternating pots of baby's tears (*Soleirolia soleirolii*) in light green and dark green or some white Impatiens.

3 For a modern look, paint the walls ocher, pale terracotta, or turquoise and fix shelves to the walls with stainless-steel store fixtures. Use bright plastic or metal containers and bold planting—huge-leafed hostas and New Guinea hybrid Impatiens in hot tropical scarlet, orange, or magenta.

Shrubs

In small spaces you need to choose shrubs that will earn their keep, by having either attractive foliage, a very long flowering period, or several seasons of interest—flowers and attractive berries in winter, perhaps, or vibrant autumn color. These are good value, even in their first year, and will go on getting even better.

Lavatera 'Barnsley'
Tree mallow

SIZE AFTER ONE SEASON:
5 feet x 3 feet

ULTIMATE SIZE:
6 x 6 feet

ZONES:
5—9

This shrub is an excellent temporary space filler, producing masses of open pale pink flowers with a red eye from early summer to the first frosts. It also has gray-green medium-sized leaves, which are a good foil for the showier flowers. Lavatera is best cut back in the spring, removing all the wood that carried flowers the previous summer, to keep it in check and to encourage better flowering. After a few years, though, it has a tendency to sprawl untidily, so take it out.

Cornus alba 'Elegantissima'
Red-stem dogwood

SIZE AFTER ONE SEASON:
5 feet x 4 feet

ULTIMATE SIZE:
10 x 13 feet

ZONES:
2—8

Red-stem dogwoods are useful shrubs for small gardens since they have more than one season of interest and can easily be kept in check. They are grown primarily for their winter bark, which in this case is rich ruby-red. In spring and summer it has pale green-and-white variegated leaves, which make it a very good background plant for other shrubs or perennials, or even a host for a small-flowered clematis. Since the brightest colored bark is produced by the previous summer's new growth, cut it hard back to about 6 inches from the ground every spring. This also encourages larger, more strikingly variegated leaves, as well as restricting the shrub's overall size. It does well on all soils, including boggy ones, and will cope with full sun to medium shade.

Chaenomeles speciosa
Chinese flowering quince

**SIZE AFTER
ONE SEASON:**
10 x 10 inches

ULTIMATE SIZE:
8 x 8 feet

ZONES:
4—9

For a glorious burst of early-spring color, plant a Chinese flowering quince. Beginning in March, in northern climes, and even earlier in warm zones, exquisite little red flowers, similar in form to apple blossoms, appear on its bare stems; some cultivars have double flowers. The flowers (which attract bees) are followed by glossy bronze, then green leaves and by the tart greenish-yellow quinces, which can be used to make jam or jelly.

Chaenomeles is not very fast-growing— about 8 inches a year—so buy one that has already achieved a good size. It will tolerate most soils, including dry ones, but prefers a slightly acidic one and a position in full sun. The taller varieties make a good hedge or can be trained espalier-like against a wall. For the best display of flowers, prune it hard every few years.

Setting standards

If you've inherited an overgrown back garden with some big old shrubs that are taking up too much room, instead of ripping them out, try "standardizing" them—removing the lower branches so that you are left with a bare trunk and growth at the top, like a tree, and more space below.

Herbaceous perennials

Many herbaceous perennials, especially those that flower in late summer and early fall, give a good show in their first season. For immediate impact, grow three, five, or, if space allows, seven plants of the same type in a group.

Knautia macedonica
Plume poppy

SIZE AFTER ONE SEASON:
6 x 2 feet

ZONES:
5—9

This plant, with its wine red cloverlike flowers, is especially valued for its long summer flowering season. It spreads with abandon so to keep it a good compact shape, grow it in well-drained, not-too-fertile soil and in full sun.

Cynara cardunculus
Cardoon

**SIZE AFTER
ONE SEASON:**
8 x 4 feet

ZONES:
6—9

This relative of the artichoke makes a dramatic temporary miniature tree substitute, with huge jagged silver leaves up to 24 inches long and vivid purple thistle flowers in summer, about the size of a grapefruit. It dies down in the fall, but will produce fresh growth the following spring. Since it takes up a lot of room, in a small space it is probably most useful as a one-season wonder. It prefers a sunny position and fertile, well-drained soil, and because of its height, it needs shelter from strong winds.

Artemisia absinthium
'Lambrook Silver'

SIZE AFTER ONE SEASON:
18 x 18 inches

ULTIMATE SIZE:
2 x 2 feet

ZONES:
3—7

This is a superb foliage plant for a sunny border. With its very finely divided bright silver foliage, it is an ideal foil both for soft pastels and for "hot" shades. Unlike other artemisias, which have rather dirty yellow flowers that are best cut off when the buds appear, this has tiny gray flowers, which you do not really notice. It likes a well-drained, but not dry, soil and full sun. If you cut it back hard in spring, you will be rewarded with new, even brighter silver foliage.

✩ *Crambe cordifolia*

SIZE AFTER ONE SEASON:
6 x 3 feet

ULTIMATE SIZE:
8 x 5 feet

ZONES:
6—8

Another huge, dramatic plant, which produces a massive cloud of tiny, fragrant white flowers from a clump of large architectural deep green leaves. Bees love it. It is best as a temporary plant in a small border, though lovely with roses where there is more space.

Ground-cover plants

These spread quickly to cover the soil, which not only gives a new garden a mature look but also helps to suppress weeds. They are best planted in groups of three, five, or seven. They will soon knit together to form an impenetrable carpet.

Campanula poscharskyana 'E. H. Frost'

SIZE AND SPREAD AFTER ONE SEASON:
6 x 16 inches

ULTIMATE SIZE:
8 inches x 3 feet

ZONES:
5—7

This forms mounds of fresh green leaves from which long growths are produced; these cover the ground very quickly but give it a reputation for invasiveness. However, it is very easily controlled by simply pulling off the growths when they have gone too far. It grows in sun or part-shade and in most soil types except very boggy ones. It will also grow in cracks in paving or walls.

Galium odoratum
Sweet woodruff

SIZE AFTER ONE SEASON:
6 x 18 inches

ULTIMATE SIZE:
6 inches x indefinite

ZONES:
5—8

This excellent ground-cover plant grows very quickly sideways, soon forming a carpet of pretty, fresh, green lobed leaves. It is usually deciduous, but in my own temperate garden it keeps its leaves all winter. In late spring and early summer it has scented white, starry flowers. It will carry on spreading, so either give it plenty of room or chop it back with a spade when it overreaches itself. As a woodland plant, it likes moist soil and dappled shade. It is good used formally, in a circular brick-edged bed, for example, or informally as weed-suppressing ground cover under shrubs or trees.

Grasses

An excellent group of plants for the impatient landscaper because they grow very quickly but, except in a few cases, are not invasive. They have a very long season of interest—even the dead stems of deciduous grasses look great in winter—and they are also good in containers.

Calamagrostis x *acutiflora* 'Karl Foerster'

SIZE AFTER ONE SEASON:
6 x 1 foot

ULTIMATE SIZE:
6 x 2 foot

ZONES:
5—9

This very upright grass with fine medium-green leaves is excellent for providing height without bulk. In early summer it has brownish pink flowers that gradually fade to buff. The dead stems and foliage turn an attractive pale gold and give valuable structure through the winter. They look marvelous with the frost on them, illuminated by the low winter sun. Cut back the dead growth as soon as new shoots start appearing in early spring.

Miscanthus sinensis 'Silberfeder'

SIZE AFTER ONE SEASON: 6 x 1 foot

ULTIMATE SIZE: 8 x 4 feet

ZONES: 4—9

An attractive grass with slender arching medium-green leaves, this produces upright silvery flower heads in late summer/early fall, which may stay on the plant through the winter and add valuable structure to the garden. Cut all the dead growth down in early spring. Miscanthus prefers sun and a moist but free-draining soil. It can cope with drier soil but does not thrive when it is too wet.

Helictotrichon sempervirens
Blue oat grass

**SIZE AFTER
ONE SEASON:**
2 x 2¹/₂ feet

ULTIMATE SIZE:
2 x 2¹/₂ feet

ZONES:
4—9

This gracefully arching blue-green foliage of blue oat grass is evergreen, and within a year will reach its full height of 2 feet or more—two qualities that make it an excellent choice for the impatient landscaper. In early summer it produces pale golden yellow flowers on long stems. It has a neat habit, forming dense, rounded clumps, and works well either by itself or as part of a border. Although it prefers full sun, it doesn't mind partial shade. Poor to moderately fertile, alkaline soil suits it best.

Bulbs

These are great for impatient landscapers because you can buy many of them already in flower in pots and can see immediately what you are getting. Remove the clump carefully from its pot and plant it in the ground or in a decorative container, or simply bury the pot and then, once the flowering is over, plant the bulbs in the soil. Or plant spring-flowering bulbs in fall for a great show a few months later.

Allium christophii

**SIZE AFTER
ONE SEASON:**
2 feet x 6 inches

ULTIMATE SIZE:
2 feet x 6 inches

ZONES:
4—8

Alliums certainly add drama to any border. This particular variety produces long, slender stems supporting large heads the size of a grapefruit in late spring and early summer. The heads are made up of masses of small, silvery-mauve starlike flowers. Once the flowers die, the heads fade to a soft golden beige color. They are very attractive still, so are well worth leaving on the plant until they crumble. These alliums need a reasonably free-draining soil and a sunny position. They take up very little ground space, so are ideal for growing among other plants.

Iris reticulata

**SIZE AFTER
ONE SEASON:**
4–6 x 2 inches

ZONES:
5—8

This is a very attractive miniature iris with deep blue velvety flowers with a splash of gold on each petal. In mild climates, it can start flowering as early as January. It looks terrific growing through low ground-cover plants such as epimedium or evergreen vinca. It is also very attractive en masse in pots.

Narcissus 'Hawera'

**SIZE IN ONE
SEASON:**
10 x 3 inches

ZONES:
4—8

There are many superb dwarf daffodils
suitable for small gardens or containers,
but this is one of my favorites, producing
nodding clusters of canary yellow flowers
in late spring. Plant en masse for the best
effect, and leave the foliage to die down
for six weeks after flowering is over, so
that it can manufacture food for the bulb
to produce next year's flowers. Planting
these daffodils under deciduous shrubs or
among perennials will hide the dying
foliage or at least distract the eye.

Annuals

Annuals grow, flower, set seed, and die in one season and so are great for quick and easy color in a new garden or in existing borders that are lacking cohesion. Hardy annuals, which are sown directly into the soil, are very easy to grow and can be in flower in 10–12 weeks. You can buy half-hardy annuals as plants, but they should not go outside until all danger of frost has past.

Calendula 'Indian Prince'
Pot marigold

SIZE IN ONE SEASON: 18–24 x 10 inches

One of the very fastest annuals to flower from seed—in about eight weeks—this is a favorite for informal gardens. This variety has deep orange flowers and looks marvelous on its own or grown with deep blues such as love-in-a-mist and cornflowers. Its flowers are edible and add a real visual zing to a salad. It self-seeds very easily.

Tepee effect

Make a tall tepee of copper piping tied at the top with a leather thong or strong jute, and stand it in the border. This will become a dramatic focal point right away. Around the base, sow bright orange California poppy (*Eschscholzia californica*) seed. Once all danger of frost is past, plant rich blue morning glories (*Ipomoea tricolor* 'Heavenly Blue'), bought as young plants from the garden center, at the base of each leg, and encourage them to latch on. By midsummer they should be producing a profusion of lovely trumpet flowers, each one lasting only for a morning—hence the plant's common name.

Helianthus annuus
Sunflower

SIZE IN ONE SEASON
6 x 1 foot

The best fast annual there is; and, grown en masse, it is a great and stylish space filler. As well as the classic giant yellow variety, look for the rich mahogany *H. a.* 'Velvet Queen', or the very pale lemon *H. a.* 'Italian White', both slightly smaller at around 5 feet. Sow the seeds directly in soil or in planting mix in a large pot in mid-spring.

Nigella damascena 'Miss Jekyll'
Love-in-a-mist

SIZE IN ONE SEASON:
18 x 6 inches

This is one of the best and easiest hardy annuals, with very fine, feathery foliage and rich blue flowers, followed by golden brown seed capsules, which look like precious stones in an ornate filigree setting. It likes a sunny position. Another rampant self-seeder, it can be sown in the fall for an earlier show the following year.

Basket case

If you have an old tree in your garden, one very quick and easy way of brightening up the whole area is to suspend several hanging baskets from the branches. For maximum impact, make the baskets identical and stick to a limited color range. This color scheme is orange and yellow.

❀ Line a 14-inch plastic-coated wire basket with moss and fill with soilless potting mix mixed with water-retaining gel crystals and controlled-release fertilizer. Plant with three *Lysimachia nummularia* 'Aurea', three *Lysimachia congestiflora* 'Outback Sunset'®, three *Bidens ferulifolia*, five *Zinnia* 'Profusion Orange', and ten nasturtium plants—*Tropaeolum majus* 'Tip Top Apricot'. In addition, push ten or so nasturtium seeds into the mix. These will start flowering later in the summer and will help keep the whole glorious display going for longer. Finally, at the center use a foliage plant—*Artemisia vulgaris* 'Oriental Limelight'. Water every day and twice a day in hot weather.

Instant plants

These plants are worth buying as large, mature specimens, because they will establish well and give your garden instant height and drama.

Hosta sieboldiana var. *elegans*

SIZE AFTER 2/3 SEASONS:
18 x 18 inches

ULTIMATE SIZE:
3 x 4 feet

ZONES:
4—8

Of the hundreds of hostas available, this is one of the most spectacular, with its huge rounded, ribbed blue-green leaves and tall spikes of pale lilac flowers in early summer. One large plant or a matching pair makes a stunning, instant focal point. It likes deep, rich soil that never dries out and will grow in sun or part-shade. The more moisture it has, the more sun it can take.

Phyllostachys nigra
Black bamboo

ZONES:
7—10

A large specimen of this bamboo makes an eye-catching focal point or screen.

Pyracantha
Firethorn

SIZE AFTER
2/3 SEASONS:
6 x 4 feet

ULTIMATE SIZE:
13 x 10 feet

ZONES:
5—9

This useful evergreen wall shrub offers a long season of interest, retaining its glossy, dark green foliage (in warmer zones) throughout the winter. Pretty white clusters of flowers in the spring are followed by masses of yellow, orange, or scarlet berries, which last well into fall or even winter—or until the birds get them. It is happy in everything from full sun to deep shade, although it will flower less freely in the latter; but it dislikes very exposed positions.

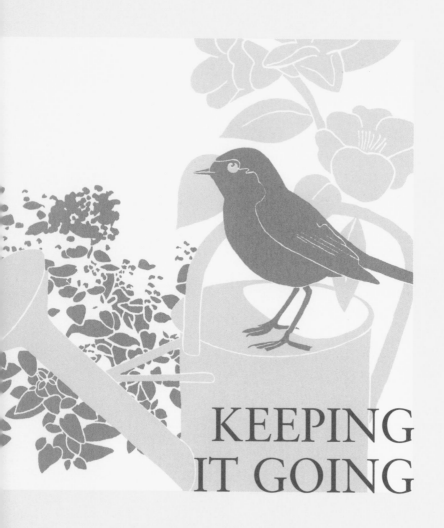

KEEPING
IT GOING

Impatient Landscaper's Questions

Q *I'm an impatient landscaper, so time is precious and I'd rather entertain, relax, or sit in my garden than slave away in it. How can I avoid all those tedious garden chores?*

A The trick is to identify the routine tasks that take up most time, and either eliminate them altogether, or reduce them to a bare minimum.

Seven tips to minimize weeding

1 As with so many things, prevention is better than cure. If you are planting a garden from scratch, dig the soil over very thoroughly and remove every scrap of weed root. Many weeds will grow from even $^1/_{16}$ inch of root. Remember the old saying "One year's seed, seven years' weeds." Remove weeds before they set seed.

2 If the problem starts in a neighboring garden, you need to make a barrier. Dig a trench about 12 inches deep along the base of the fence on your side, then nail a 12-inch-wide strip of thick black plastic sheet along the bottom of the fence and push it down into the trench. This will prevent most perennial weeds from creeping under the fence and into your garden.

3 Mulch. Once the soil is as free from perennial weeds as possible, keep them at bay by covering the soil with a layer of mulch.

4 Choose either an organic material such as compost, cocoa shells, or composted bark, or an inorganic mulch of gravel, stone chips, or even crushed glass.

5 Alternatively, lay a woven membrane over the soil and cover this with a purely ornamental layer of gravel or bark.

6 Use ground-cover plants. In the longer term these are an attractive way of keeping weeds under control.

7 As a last resort, if you don't want to do the weeding yourself, get an experienced landscaper in.

Four tips to minimize watering

1 Mulch (again!) Apply a mulch when the soil is already moist and it will help keep moisture in.

2 Install an automatic watering system. The simplest consists of a soaker hose—a porous pipe that slowly seeps water along its entire length. Lay it permanently on the soil around the base of shrubs and trees and weave it in and out of the smaller plants. You can cover it with soil or with a mulch. Attach it to a water computer fixed to an outside tap to set watering times.

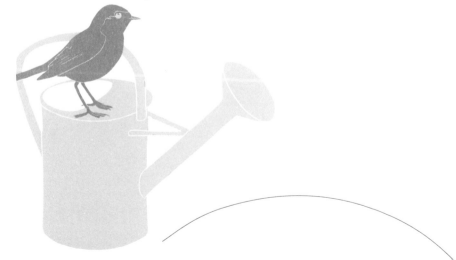

3 For containers, you need a micro-irrigation system—a feeder hose into which much narrower plastic pipes are fixed. These have either a drip feeder or a small spray on a spike at the other end. The spikes are then pushed into the soil and the water is delivered exactly where it is needed. This system can also be controlled by a water computer.

4 Reduce the amount of watering needed by plants in containers by mixing water-retaining gel crystals into the potting mix as you plant. These are able to hold many times their own volume of water, which they then release gradually into the mix.

Feed me

* For a garden you are starting from scratch, dig in some decent organic matter such as well-rotted manure or compost. Use only one shovelful of manure every square yard and two shovelfuls of compost. Adding a little bit extra in the hope of making your plants grow even faster will only produce lots of soft sappy growth that is prone to all sorts of pests and diseases.

* If you are planting in an existing border, mix organic matter into the soil at the bottom of the planting hole and into the soil with which you refill the hole.

❀ If you are not concerned about being organic, you can use an inorganic fertilizer. The easiest to use are controlled-release fertilizers that last a whole season and can be used in borders or for containers. These come as granules or thimble-shaped plugs, which you simply push into the soil or into the potting mix in your containers. The coating of the granules is heat sensitive. The granules start to release their nutrients only when the soil or potting mix warms up and the plants start to grow and need feeding, so you can also use them if you plant in the fall.

Impatient Landscaper's Questions

Q *Do I really have to do all that pruning stuff I've read about in books?*

A Pruning isn't that difficult, but it helps to understand why you need to prune. First of all, it keeps plants within the space allotted to them. You could grow only plants that will remain very small, but that would be boring. For the sake of fifteen minutes or so once a year—all it takes to prune most plants—isn't it more fun to grow some bigger, much more exciting specimens and keep them under control?

The second reason for pruning is that it removes some of the old, tired wood. Most shrubs flower more freely on younger wood and produce larger flowers, too. And for shrubs that feature colored leaves and bark, pruning will produce bigger and more intensely colored leaves and brighter bark.

Q *But isn't there a risk I'll kill the plants?*

A It's very hard to kill a plant by pruning it. Tests have shown that even if you prune a rose with a hedge trimmer from time to time, it will still flower well, though it may not be a beautiful shape. In general, the worst that is likely to happen is that if you prune at the wrong time of year you will lose that season's flowers.

All you need to know to prune spring and early-summer flowerers

✿ These flower on growth they made the previous summer, so they need to be pruned immediately they have finished flowering.

✿ They will spend the rest of the summer producing the wood on which next year's flowers will form.

✿ Cut back all of the growth that has borne flowers to the point from which a healthy new shoot is emerging.

All you need to know to prune plants that flower from midsummer onward

🌸 These produce flowers on growth made this year, so the old growth needs to be pruned back hard in late fall after flowering or, better still, in very early spring just as the plants start growing.

🌸 If you don't prune, you will get flowers high up, on the new season's growth, and the flowers will be smaller and fewer, too.

All you need to know about pruning roses

🌸 Just remove any dead, diseased or very weak and spindly growth.

🌸 When you deadhead, always remove 6—8 inches of stem at the same time. This helps to keep the rose in check.

✿ Cut out an older stem or two right down to ground level in early spring every few years to encourage strong new growth from the base.

✿ And best of all, avoid planting roses that need extensive annual pruning—primarily the hybrid teas or floribundas. Instead choose more easily maintained types such as modern shrub roses, English roses, and patio roses.

Index